THE GOOD, THE BAD, THE SLIMY

THE SECRET LIFE OF MICROBES

Acknowledgements
Many thanks to Tamar Barkay and James Bricker for reading the manuscript with their expert eyes;
any errors are mine and may be placed at my doorstep. And as always,
thanks to my family, Tony, Alison, Caitlin, and Eli, for their love and support. — S.L.L.

Thanks to Chris Porter of Chris Porter Illustration for colorizations
of Dennis Kunkel's elecronic micrographs. — D.K.

Library of Congress Cataloging-in-Publication Data

Latta, Sara L.
  The good, the bad, the slimy : the secret life of microbes / Sara L. Latta.— 1st ed.
    p. cm.
  Includes bibliographical references and index.
  ISBN-10: 0-7660-1294-8
  1. Microorganisms—Juvenile literature. 2. Bacteria—Juvenile literature. 3. Microbiology—Juvenile literature.
I. Title.
  QR57.L38 2005
  579—dc22   2005035405

ISBN-13: 978-0-7660-1294-3

Printed in the United States of America

10 9 8 7 6 5 4 3 2

To Our Readers: We have done our best to make sure all Internet Addresses in this book were active and appropriate when we went to press. However, the author and the publisher have no control over and assume no liability for the material available on those Internet sites or on other Web sites they may link to. Any comments or suggestions can be sent by e-mail to comments@enslow.com or to the address on the back cover.

Photo Credits: All photos Copyright © Dennis Kunkel Microscopy, Inc., except as follows: © 2006 Jupiterimages Corporation, pp. 33 (inset), 34, 37 (inset), 44, 47, 48, 55, 60, 61, 63, 69; B. Murton / Southamption Oceanography Centre / Photo Researchers, Inc., p. 101; CDC, p. 94; © Corel Corporation, p. 87; Courtesy of the National Museum of Health and Medicine, Armed Forces Institute of Pathology, Washington, D.C. (#Ncp 1603), pp. 70–71; David Nunuk / Photo Researchers, Inc., pp. 102–103; Dr. Jeremy Burgess / Photo Researchers, Inc., p. 40 (background); ESA-D. Ducros, pp. 96–97, 110; European Space Agency (ESA)/DLR/FU Berlin (G. Neukum), pp. 99, 109; Gregory G. Dimijian, M.D. / Photo Researchers, Inc., p. 21 (inset); J. William Schopf, UCLA, p. 50; Library of Congress, pp. 10, 84, 88; Michael Abbey / Photo Researchers, Inc., p. 33 (background); National Library of Medicine, pp. 78, 81 (inset); National Oceanic and Atmospheric Administration, pp. 73, 74; National Park Service, p. 15; © Ned Therrien / Visuals Unlimited, p. 46; NASA/JPL/University of Arizona, pp. 112–113; Pfizer Corporation, p. 64; Sidney Moulds / Photo Researchers, p. 17 (inset)

Cover Photos: © Dennis Kunkel Microscopy, Inc.

A Note About the Photos: Dennis Kunkel's photographs are called electron micrographs because they were taken with an electron microscope, which can magnify an object up to a million times. Electron microscopes use an electron beam with focusing magnets to produce a black-and-white photo. Most of the photos in this book were taken with a scanning electron microscope. A computer program can then be used to add colors to the subject. The colors used do not show the true colors of the subject. Colors are often used to highlight interesting features and make them easier for people to see.

The letter x at the bottom of each photograph indicates magnification. For example, x250 means the object in the picture is 250 times larger than its real size.

THE GOOD, THE BAD, THE SLIMY

THE SECRET LIFE OF MICROBES

Sara L. Latta

Photographs by Dennis Kunkel, Ph.D.

Enslow Publishers, Inc.
40 Industrial Road
Box 398
Berkeley Heights, NJ 07922
USA

http://www.enslow.com

Contents

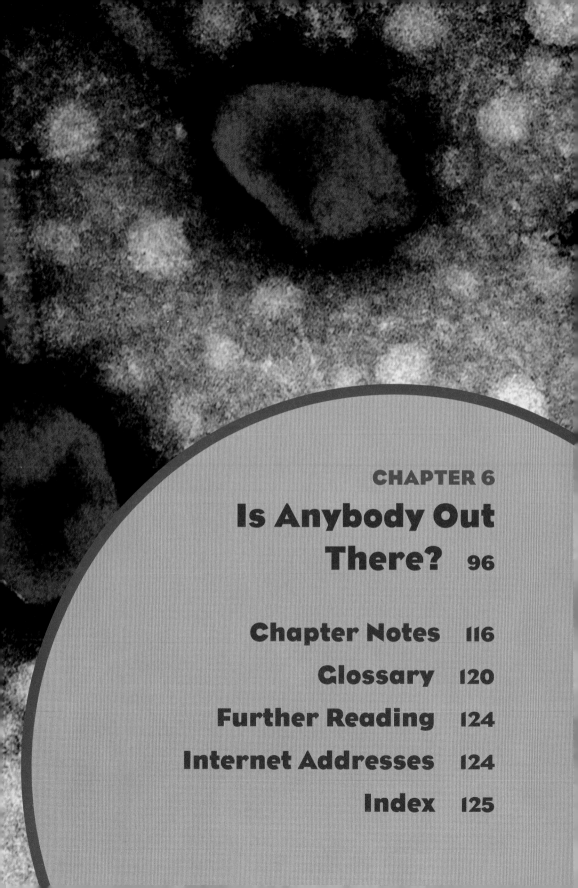

CHAPTER 1
Invisible World

Suppose you drank a magic potion that made all of the human cells in your body invisible. What would your friends see? A ghostly, shimmering zoo of **microbes**, that's what! Your body—from the top of your head to the tips of your toes and nearly everywhere in between—is home to trillions and trillions of **bacteria, fungi**, and other things too small to see without a microscope. Incredibly, the bacterial cells in our bodies outnumber our human cells about ten to one![1] And that's only the beginning.

Earth—perhaps even other planets—is teeming with life that we cannot see with our eyes alone. This book will show you the secret life of the microscopic living things we call microbes.

• • •

In 1683, a Dutch merchant and amateur microscope maker wrote about a mysterious new world filled with strange creatures. He saw "many very small animalcules. . . . The

Mold used to make cheese (x975)

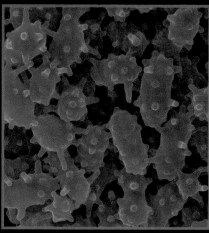

Bacteria found in soil and in human intestinal tract (x8,625)

largest sort . . . [was] leaping about in the
fluid, like the fish called a Jack. . . . The sec-
ond sort . . . had a . . . whirling motion." A
third kind of creature moved like "gnats, or
flies sporting in the air."[2]

Protozoan with hair-like cilia
coming out of its mouth
(x2,040)

Dust mite (x520)

Athlete's foot fungus (x1,750)

This Dutch merchant, Antoni van Leeuwenhoek (LAY wen hook), was the first person to observe microscopic life. The "little animals" described above came from the plaque

between his teeth, but Leeuwenhoek also discovered tiny creatures living in lake water, on cheese, and even in his own bowel movements!

Antoni van Leeuwenhoek first saw microscopic life when he examined his own tooth plaque in 1683.

What Are Microbes?

The simplest definition of a microbe is a living thing, or **organism**, too tiny to be seen without the aid of a microscope. Most—but not all—are a single cell. They fall into five categories: **bacteria**, **archaea**, **fungi**, **protists**, and **viruses**.

TABLE I
HOW LIVING THINGS ARE CLASSIFIED

Prokaryotes

are one-celled organisms. They have no **nucleus**.

Eukaryotes may

be either one-celled or many-celled organisms. They have a nucleus.

BACTERIA
Cyanobacterium

(x5,335)

ARCHAEA
Halobacterium

(x1,600)

PROTISTS
diatom

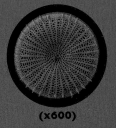

(x600)

FUNGI
green mold

(x220)

ANIMALS
deer tick

(x12)

PLANTS
ragweed pollen

(x340)

Viruses are in a category of their own. They are not true cells, but tiny bundles of **DNA** or **RNA** inside a protein coat. They rely on other organisms to reproduce.

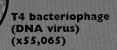

T4 bacteriophage
(DNA virus)
(x55,065)

Not all eukaryotes are microbes; plants and animals also belong to this group.

Leeuwenhoek thought that "among all the marvels that I have discovered in nature, [these are] the most marvelous of all."

Bacteria

As Leeuwenhoek observed, not all bacteria look the same, although all of them are basically one of three different shapes. Some, like the microbes used to make yogurt (*Lactobacillus*), are rod-shaped. Others, such as *Staphylococcus aureus* (a common skin bacterium), are round. Still others, including a disease-causing organism called *Leptospira interrogans*, are spiral, like a corkscrew. Bacteria can form groups called **colonies**. Some of these colonies are beautiful and can easily be seen with the naked eye.

Just as animals range in size from a tiny hummingbird to the giant blue whale, bacteria come in different sizes, too. Bacteria called *Mycoplasmas* are so small they were once believed to be viruses. The world's largest known bacteria, *Thiomargarita namibiensis*, were found in the ocean floor off the coast of Africa. Each cell is about the size of the period at the end of this sentence.

Bacteria come in three different shapes: round, rod-shaped, and spiral (x6,425).

What's in a Name?

Related species (specific kinds) of organisms can be classified into a genus. Each different type of organism within that genus has a species name. For example, the house cat belongs to the genus *Felis* and the species *domestica*. Its Latin name is *Felis domestica*. The lion also belongs to the genus *Felis*, but its species name is *leo: Felis leo*. Microbes are also classified this way.

13

Some bacteria have whiplike structures called flagella that act like tiny motors to propel them through their liquid environments. Others glide along surfaces by secreting slimy chemicals.

Archaea

Yellowstone National Park is famous for geysers such as Old Faithful, bubbling mudpots, and colorful hot springs. The hot springs are home to many kinds of archaea as well as some heat-loving bacteria. They thrive in conditions that would kill most other organisms. One of the first archaeons to be discovered, *Sulfolobus*, lives in near-boiling conditions in some Yellowstone hot springs. It eats hydrogen sulfide (the stuff that smells like rotten eggs) and makes acid.

Some archaea live in hot **hydrothermal vents** at the bottom of the ocean. Others are buried deep in Antarctic ice. The word *archaea* comes from the Greek word meaning "ancient." It is a fitting name, because many archaea live in conditions much like those when the first life emerged on Earth, more than 3.5 billion years ago. Earth was probably very hot then—the

Yellowstone National Park is famous for its geysers and hot springs. In the Grand Prismatic Spring, mats of colored microbes cause the oranges, reds, greens, and yellows, while the bright blue color is refracted sunlight.

oceans regularly reached the boiling point— and there was no oxygen. Some scientists think of archaea as living fossils, providing important clues to the **evolution** of life on Earth.

Under the microscope, archaea look a lot like bacteria. In fact, scientists once thought they were a weird kind of bacteria. But when scientists looked more closely at the **genome** of these strange organisms, they weren't like bacteria at all. In fact, they seemed to more closely related to you and me than to bacteria!

Fungi

Why did they invite the mushroom to the party? Because he was a fungi (pronounced FUN guy)!

Fungi include microbes such as yeasts and molds. However, mushrooms and some other types of fungi are not microbes. Yeasts—including those used to make bread rise—are single-celled creatures that exist individually. They are round or oval, and although they are too small to be seen as individual cells, you can see colonies of them growing together.

If you've ever forgotten a sandwich in the bottom of your locker, you've probably seen fuzzy stuff growing on the bread. These are colonies of molds. The organism that makes the **antibiotic** penicillin is also a mold.

Protists

The protists are a motley collection of living things. One group of protists is the **protozoans**. *Protozoan* means "first animals." Like many animals, they have to hunt and catch their food—mostly other microbes. Not

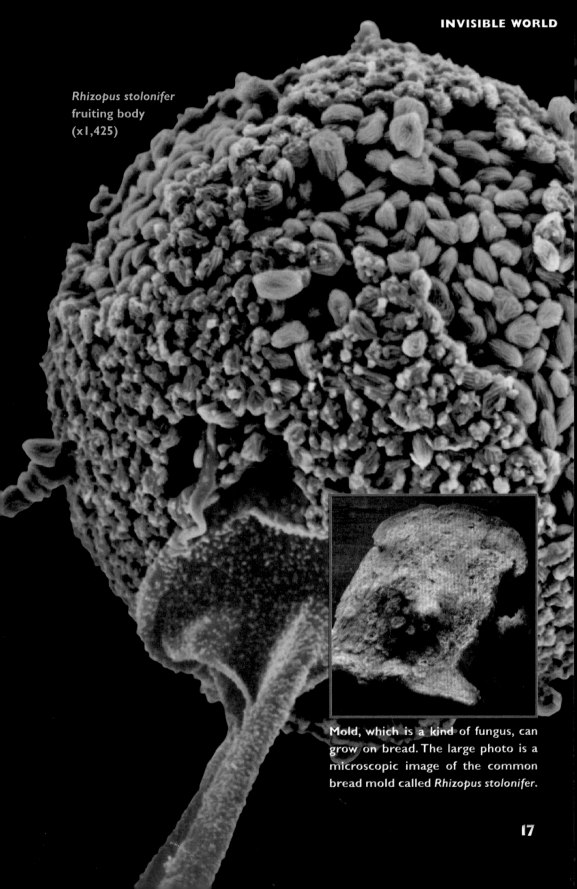

Rhizopus stolonifer
fruiting body
(x1,425)

Mold, which is a kind of fungus, can grow on bread. The large photo is a microscopic image of the common bread mold called *Rhizopus stolonifer*.

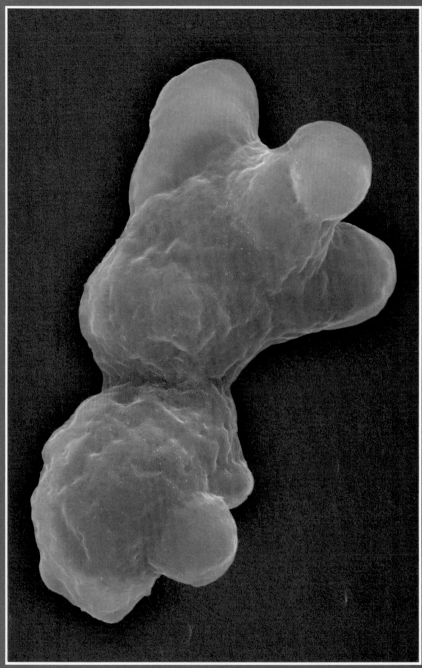

This amoeba, called *Entamoeba histolytica*, causes intestinal diseases (x3,150).

surprisingly, most can move. Amoebas, microbial jellylike blobs, ooze about by extending their stretchy cell membranes, forming "pseudopods" (false feet). Other protozoans are covered with little bristles (cilia) or sport whip-like tails (flagella) that help them move about.

A *Paramecium* is a protozoan. The cilia that cover its body help it move (x300).

Most protozoans live in water or other moist places, including inside the bodies of animals. Scientists have found protozoans in oceans, lakes, streams, and in the soil. Most protozoans are harmless, but some can cause serious diseases, including malaria and a life-threatening type of diarrhea called dysentery.

Algae are another kind of protist. The stringy stuff that grows in lakes and rivers and some forms of seaweed are algae. There are also microscopic forms of algae in fresh and salt water, on damp rocks, on tree trunks, and in soil. Like plants, algae use the sun's energy to make food. This process is called **photosynthesis**. Algae and other photosynthetic microbes make as much as half of the oxygen that we breathe![3]

In 1958, a science fiction movie called *The Blob* featured an alien life form that consumed everything in its path. The inspiration for the movie? The slime mold—another kind of protist. (In real life, slime molds generally stick to eating rotting plants, such as dead logs and leaves.)

When food is plentiful, slime molds exist as individual microscopic cells. Things get interesting when food is scarce, however. The individual cells come together to form a mass that

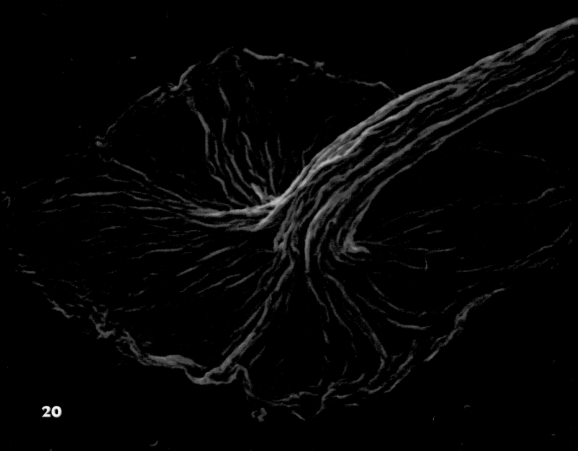

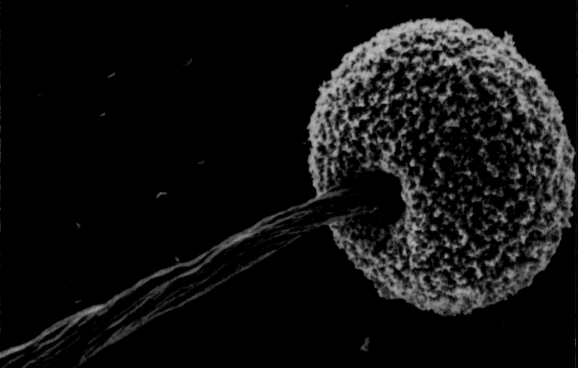

can resemble foam, jelly, . . . or "The Blob."
One slime mold has been described as looking
like dog vomit. The whole blob can move, like
an amoeba, in search of food.

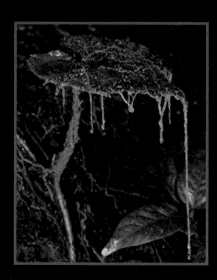

Slime mold grows over a
wet log and leaves. The mold
grows one centimeter (half
an inch) per hour. The large
photo shows what a slime
mold's fruiting body looks
like under a microscope
(x270).

Viruses

Viruses are not cells. In fact, they are kind of like the zombies of the microbial world. They're not living, technically speaking, but they're not a mere collection of chemicals, either. They are simply packages of genetic information. By themselves, they can't take in nutrients or get rid of waste. They can't even reproduce.

But once a virus lands on the right type of cell, it can do one of two things. Some viruses trick the host cell into swallowing them up. Other viruses inject their genetic information into the cell. Once inside, the virus uses the host cell to make new viruses. Some multiply rapidly, destroying the host cell and causing disease. Most known viruses, however, are not too harmful. They simply live in the host cell. They either do nothing, or they make copies of themselves at a slow and steady rate.[4]

Herpes viruses land on a blood cell inside the body. Viruses need other cells in order to make copies of themselves (x235,655).

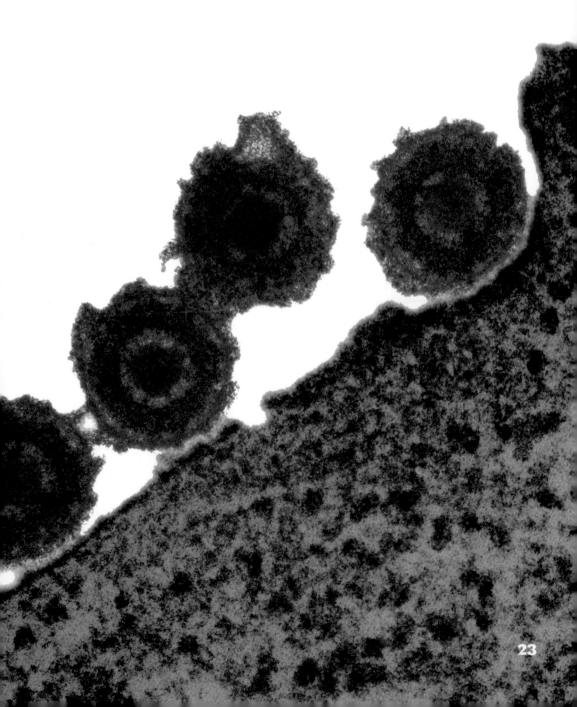

Marvelous Microbes

Today, most people think of microbes as mere germs that make them sick. While it's true that some microbes cause disease—from the common cold to **epidemics** that kill millions—most microbes are harmless. In fact, microorganisms are essential to life on Earth. Billions of years ago, microbes created the oxygen-rich air we breathe. This made it possible for more complex living things to evolve.

Friendly microbes that live in our intestines help us digest food, and they prevent disease-causing germs from invading. We use microbes to clean up hazardous waste sites, make antibiotics, and fertilize our soil. They help us make bread, cheese, chocolate and other good things to eat. Disease-causing microorganisms have influenced human evolution, shaped the development of societies, and even changed the course of history. If we ever find life on other planets, many scientists are betting that it will be—you guessed it—microbial.

Antoni Van Leeuwenhoek was right. Microbes *are* marvelous.

DNA viruses (x410,910)

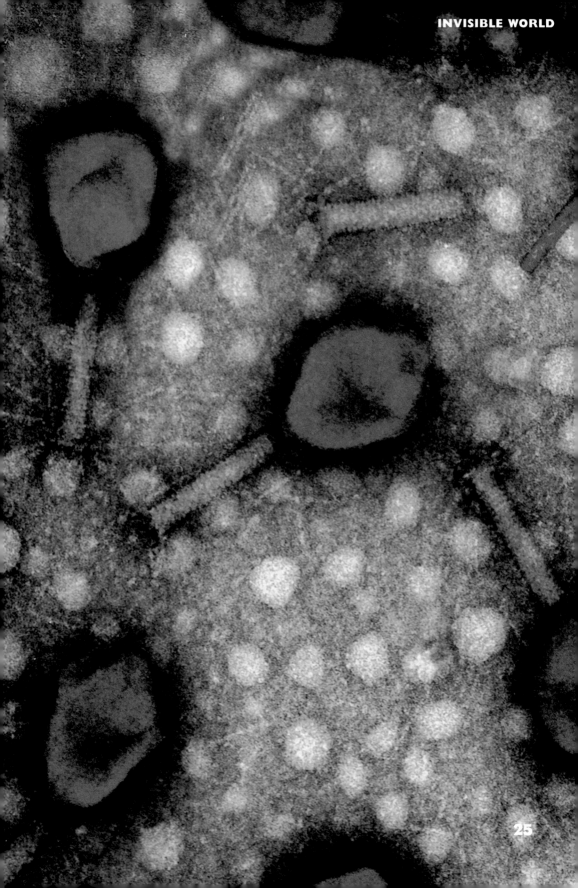

CHAPTER 2

We Are Not Alone

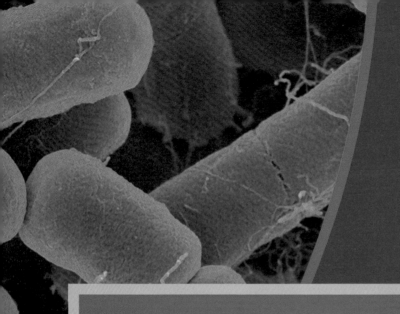

If you're lonely,
Sad and blue,
Think of all
The microbes on you.

Your relationship with microbes began the moment you were born. As you entered your mom's birth canal, microorganisms began to live on every surface of your body that is somehow connected to the outside. For example, your body is like a maze. It has entrances, like your mouth. It also has exits, such as your anus. In between, it has many twists, turns, and dead ends. Microorganisms called "normal flora" live on nearly every surface of your mazelike body.

Many of these microbes are on your side (most of the time anyway); in fact, you could not live without them. They help you digest food and they crowd out disease-causing microbes. They can sometimes be annoying, however. Our normal flora are responsible for bad breath, body odor, and farts. They can cause tooth decay and pimples. If microorganisms (even normally friendly ones) enter your blood, bones, or muscles, you could become ill.

The Inside Story

Most of the microbes that live in our bodies are packed inside our guts, especially the large intestine and the lower part of the small intestine. These good microbes help protect us against disease. They take up space and nutrients that might otherwise be used by disease-causing microbes. If the good microbes were not there, taking up room and using up food, the disease-causing microbes would have little competition. They would multiply and grow.

One beneficial kind of gut bacteria, *Bacteroides thetaiotaomicron*, helps blood vessels grow in babies. These blood vessels carry nutrients—chemicals we need to live and grow—from the gut to the rest of the body. Other types of gut bacteria also help "educate" the cells of the baby's **immune system**. They "teach" the baby's cells to tell the difference between friendly microbes and disease-causing microbes.[1]

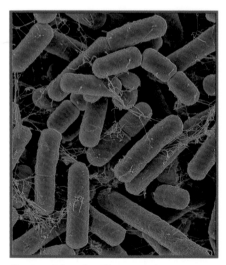

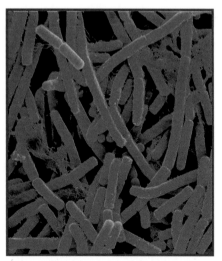

Bacteroides is the most common bacteria found in our intestines (x5,400).

These bacteria live on skin. When pores get clogged with oil, these bacteria multiply and cause pimples (x2,700).

A Thrilling Story
About *Helicobacter pylori*

Ulcers are painful sores in the lining of the stomach. Doctors once thought that they were caused by stress. Then, two Australian scientists found small, curved bacteria in the stomachs of people who had ulcers. They suggested that the disease was caused by this microbe, which was later named *Helicobacter pylori*.

"Outrageous," the scientific community said. Everybody knew that ulcers are caused by stress! And besides, it was believed that no bacterium could survive for long in the stomach's acids. In 1985, Barry J. Marshall, one of the scientists, tested himself to see if any of these microbes lived in his stomach. None did. Then, he drank a flask full of the bacteria, *H. pylori*. Sure enough, he soon developed an

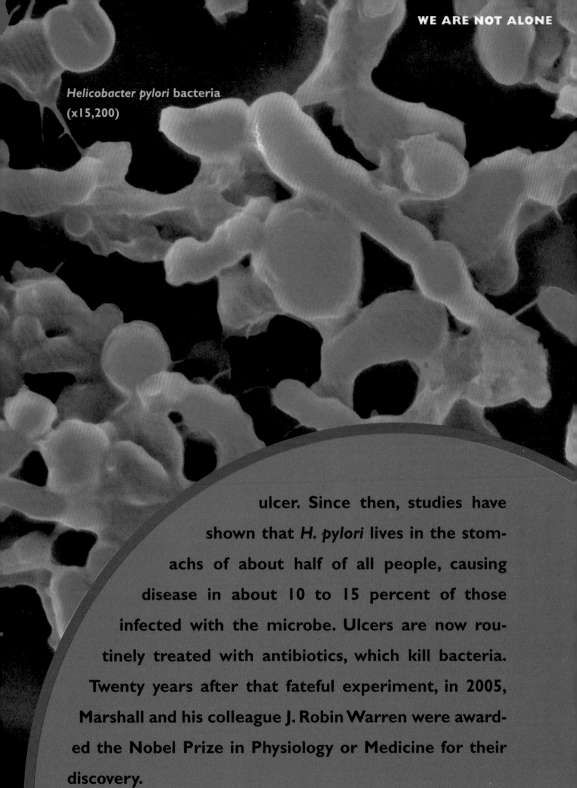

Helicobacter pylori bacteria
(x15,200)

ulcer. Since then, studies have shown that *H. pylori* lives in the stomachs of about half of all people, causing disease in about 10 to 15 percent of those infected with the microbe. Ulcers are now routinely treated with antibiotics, which kill bacteria. Twenty years after that fateful experiment, in 2005, Marshall and his colleague J. Robin Warren were awarded the Nobel Prize in Physiology or Medicine for their discovery.

31

Gut bacteria also produce many vitamins that we cannot make. They break down food, especially plant starches, that we cannot digest on our own. These starches, or **carbohydrates**, are important sources of energy and chemicals the body needs. Without these microbes, the starches would pass, unused, through our bodies.

There is almost no oxygen in the gut. When gut microbes break down carbohydrates in the absence of oxygen, we say they are fermenting. One of the waste products of **fermentation** is gas. The average person passes gas, or farts, about ten to fifteen times a day. Yes, it can be embarrassing, but it is a sign that your gut bacteria are happy and well fed.

Cows, Squid, and Other Homes for Microbes

Just like you, most animals and plants are homes for microbes. Many animals depend on microbes to digest their food. Take the wood-eating termite, for example. Wood is really, really hard to digest, as you might imagine. But

These protozoans live inside termites. They digest the wood that termites eat.

Termites have microbes that live in their guts.

33

Bessie's Burps and Global Warming

Some of the most common bacteria in the cow's digestive system produce **methane** gas as a waste product. This is good for the cow, but it may be a huge problem for the environment. The roughly 100 million cattle in the U.S. alone belch and fart about 5.5 million metric tons of methane into the atmosphere each year.[2] Methane and other gases (sometimes called **green-house gases**) trap more

of the sun's heat inside the atmosphere, which makes Earth warmer. This is called global warming. If it continues, it could be very harmful for life on our planet.

the termite gets help from protozoans and bacteria living in its gut. They break down the chewed-up bits of wood into **molecules** that the termite can use for energy.

Cows and other ruminants (animals that have four-part stomachs) get much of their nutrition from grass and other hard-to-digest plants. Their guts teem with different microbes. The microbes break down the tough plant material into nutrients that the animal can use.

Deep below the surface of the ocean, vents in the ocean floor spew plumes of hot water and minerals. Communities of strange creatures, including giant clams, crabs, blind shrimp, and a giant tubeworm called *Riftia pachyptila*, live near these vents. The tubeworm, which can grow up to 8 feet long, is remarkable because it has no mouth, gut, or anus. It gets all of its food and energy from bacteria that live inside its special pouch. The tubeworm provides the bacteria with chemicals that the bacteria need to live, including oxygen, **carbon dioxide**, and hydrogen sulfide. The bacteria use these ingredients to make food for the worm.[3] It's a great relationship that benefits the bacteria *and* the worm.

Beatrix and the Lichens

Beatrix Potter's first passion was not writing and illustrating children's stories such as *A Tale of Peter Rabbit*. It was science. As a child and teenager, she loved to collect and sketch plants, insects, spiders, and other animals. She became a superb nature artist. By the time she was in her early twenties, around the 1890s, she became fascinated with lichens, the crusty stuff that grows on rocks and tree trunks.

Most scientists at the time thought that lichens were a primitive kind of plant. However, a Swiss botanist had proposed that lichens were actually algae and fungi living together. Beatrix studied lichens with a microscope and became convinced that the Swiss scientist was correct. She made detailed drawings of lichens and wrote a paper demonstrating the partnership between fungi and algae. Most scientists of the time refused to accept this daring new idea—especially since it had been proposed by a woman![4]

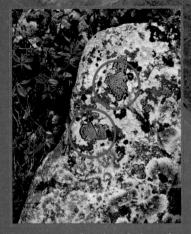

Rock lichen as seen under microsope (x490)

Lichens are fungi and algae (or fungi and cyanobacteria) that grow together on rocks. Each benefits from the other.

Today, scientists recognize that lichens are indeed a combination of a fungus with an alga or a **cyanobacterium** (or sometimes both). There are over 15,000 recognized species of lichens.

Ninety to 95 percent of a lichen's mass is a fungus. The fungus provides a sturdy structure that can cling to surfaces. The fungus makes a good home for the algae or cyanobacteria, which are enclosed within strings of the fungus. The algae or cyanobacteria capture the sun's energy to make nutrients that they share with the fungus.

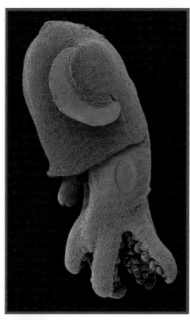

Bobtail squid have bacteria living in their body. The bacteria give off light that helps camouflage the squid (x12).

One type of squid that lives near Hawaii has formed a very different kind of partnership with a bacterium. The bobtail squid, only 4 centimeters (1.5 inches) long, comes out of its safe hiding place at dusk to look for food. A hungry fish swimming below the squid might easily look up and spot the tiny animal's outline against the moonlight above. However, the squid has some clever camouflage. It has an organ filled with bacteria. The collected bacteria give off a dim blue light, making the squid look like a shadowy burglar hidden behind a flashlight on a dark night. A newly hatched baby squid doesn't have any of these light-producing bacteria, called *Vibrio fischeri*. It must collect them from the surrounding water. The bacteria, now safe inside the squid's nutrient-rich body, soon lose the ability to live on their own.[5] Like the bacteria and the tubeworms, both organisms depend on each other for survival.

If you saw the movie *Finding Nemo*, you may remember the anglerfish. Dory and Marlin read the writing on the scuba mask by the glowing lure that dangles from his head. In real life, the anglerfish attracts its prey with a rodlike spine extending from its head; at the end of the spine is the "lure": a bulb filled with glow-in-the-dark bacteria.[6]

Dynamic Duos

Every living thing needs nitrogen, which is abundant in the air we breathe. Yet the nitrogen atoms are bonded together so tightly in air that plants, fungi, and animals can't use them. Instead, they need bacteria to take nitrogen from the air (N_2) and change it into a form that plants and other living things can use (NH_3, ammonia). This is called nitrogen fixation, because the microbes "fix" the nitrogen gas into ammonia that the plants and animals can use.

Some plants, including peanuts, clover, peas, and soybeans, have developed a partnership with nitrogen-fixing bacteria. When these plants begin to sprout and send out roots, they send out chemical signals. The signals attract the nitrogen-fixing bacteria living in the soil.

The roots form knobs around the bacteria, transporting the microbes into the heart of the root. The low-oxygen environment of the knob is perfect for the task of changing nitrogen into a form that both the plant and the bacteria can use. In return, the plant provides sugars and other nutrients that the bacteria need. It is another great partnership.

Bacteria are not the only microbes that benefit from a close association with plant roots. Most plants have a partnership with a group of fungi that wrap themselves around roots. The fungi actually become a part of the root. They send tiny strands far beyond the plant. The strands grab nutrients from the surrounding soil and send them to the plant's root. This way, the plant is reaching nutrients from farther away than its roots could reach on their own. In turn, the plant root provides the fungus with other nutrients that it needs to grow.

Some plants have roots that make knobs around bacteria. You can see these white knobs on the roots in this photo. The bacteria (inset) are able to change the nitrogen gas in the soil into a form of nitrogen that the plant and bacteria can use (x6,540).

CHAPTER 3

How Microbes Shape Our World

Here is something to think about next time you go outside: Every time you walk on the ground, you are stepping on billions of microbes. That's because there are at least one billion microbes in just one tablespoon of soil. How much is a billion? That's almost as many people as there are in China. What's more, that tablespoon probably contains at least 5,000 different kinds of microbes. This amazing

collection of bacteria, archaea, fungi, protozoa, and tiny animals plays a key role in maintaining Earth's ecosystems.

Most of these microbes are decomposers. They break dead plants and animals into smaller and smaller pieces. This makes carbon, nitrogen, and other chemical building blocks available to other living things. Dead material is turned into humus, making the soil rich with nutrients.

Many gardeners make compost from a pile of vegetable scraps, leaves, and grass clippings. The microbes in the compost heap decompose the dead things to make a rich fertilizer for flowers and vegetables.

The familiar earthy smell of soil is caused by a group of bacteria called actinomyces. They are

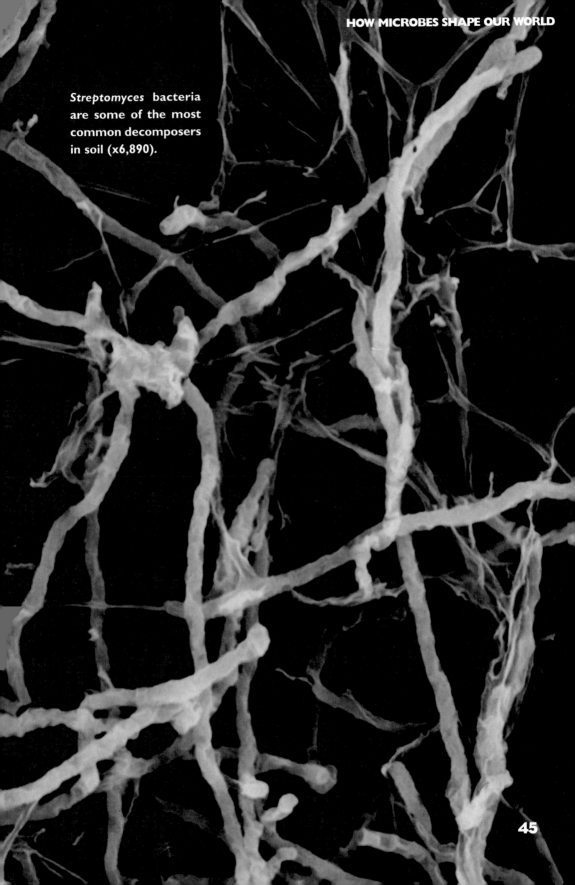

Streptomyces bacteria are some of the most common decomposers in soil (x6,890).

some of the chief decomposers in the soil. Some of these bacteria, called *Streptomyces*, also make antibiotics that we use to treat serious infections in people.

Fungi are good at decomposing really tough plant materials. They are the most efficient microbes at breaking down wood. Have you ever seen a rotting tree stump? That's evidence of fungi hard at work.

Amoebas and other protozoans are another important kind of soil microbe. They ooze along the thin film of water coating each soil particle. They eat bacteria and fungi, and their waste products help feed the soil.

Fungi cover a decaying log on the floor of a forest.

Just think of all the dead plants and animals that would pile up if there were no microbes. Over time, all of the carbon on Earth would be trapped inside dead things, and all life on Earth would come to an end. That's not a pretty picture!

Life on Earth

Microbes are Earth's chief decomposers, but they also paved the way for the formation of all life on Earth. Step back in time nearly 4.6 billion years ago. That's when Earth was a violent mass of hot, liquid rock and metal. It was surrounded by super-hot gases, steam, and near-constant flashes of lightning. The young planet was pelted with rocks from outer space—**meteorites** and **asteroids**. The first atmosphere was thick with water vapor and hydrogen, ammonia, methane, and carbon dioxide gases. There were no bodies of water on the planet, no oxygen gas—and no life. Geologists call this period the Hadean Eon. It was named after Hades, the hell of Greek mythology. But the story of the origin of Earth and the beginnings of life is no myth: It is written on ancient rocks and in the DNA of living microbes.

After many millions of years, the bombardment of asteroids and meteorites from space ended. Earth's crust and atmosphere cooled, and oceans formed from condensed water vapor. It was not yet a comfortable place for life as we know it, but for the first forms of life it was enough.

Exactly where and how life began remain a mystery. Some scientists propose that life began in warm tide pools on the surface of Earth. A growing number of scientists believe that life may have arisen deep below the surface of the ocean, near the sea vents on the ocean floor (home of the giant tubeworms you read about in Chapter 2).

Perhaps microbes came to Earth from outer space. In 1996, scientists in Antarctica discovered a meteorite from Mars. Looking at the meteorite under a microscope, they found signs that microbes might have once lived in the rock. But if there were microbes on Mars, could they have survived the trip between the two planets? Maybe. Scientists have found that lichens, which live in some of the harshest places on Earth, can even survive the extreme conditions of outer space.[1]

The First Signs of Life

In 1993, a scientist named William Schopf and his colleagues announced the discovery of microbial fossils in rocks in western Australia. The rocks were 3.5 billion years old.[2] But we know that life on Earth probably arose hundreds of millions of years before that.

By studying the genes (DNA) of modern microbes, scientists are beginning to understand what the first microbes on Earth were like. We know that those pioneering microbes did not need oxygen to survive. They probably thrived at very high temperatures. They lived off of carbon dioxide and got their energy from hydrogen and sulfur. Like the cows you read about in Chapter 2, many of these microbes made methane gas as a waste product. They filled Earth's atmosphere with methane, which traps the sun's heat inside the atmosphere. Back then, Earth needed all of the methane it could get. The sun was

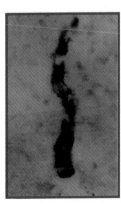

This ancient microbial fossil was found in rocks in western Australia. In the chart (right), modern (living) cyanobacteria (A,C, E, and G) are compared to fossil equivalents (B, D, F, and H). The fossils range from 850 million years old to 2,100 million years old.

CYANOBACTERIA

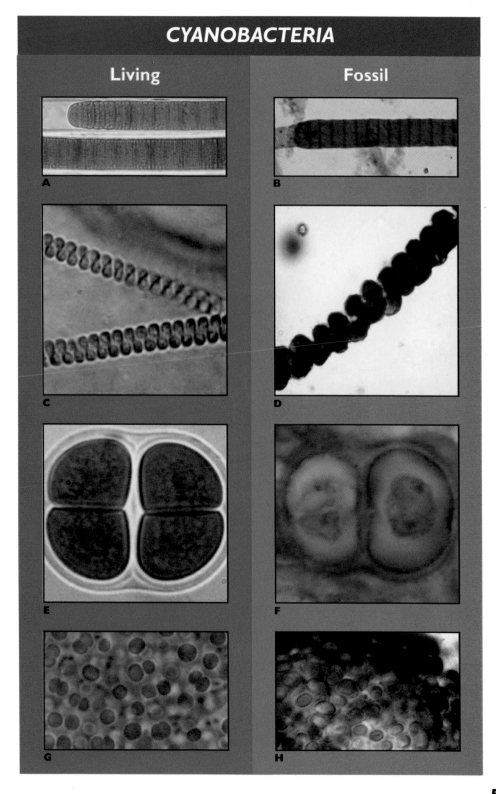

Living

Fossil

A

B

C

D

E

F

G

H

Anabaena, a cyanobacterium (x3,810)

much less bright than it is today. The Earth was in danger of becoming a ball of ice. These greenhouse gases may have kept the young Earth warm enough for life to continue evolving.[3]

Then, around 3.5 billion years ago, a new kind of microbe evolved. Called cyanobacteria, these microbes were the first to get their energy from sunlight. Unlike older microbes, they gave off oxygen gas as a waste product. Oxygen was a deadly poison for most of the other microbes. At first, much of the oxygen reacted with minerals such as iron or sulfur. But as the cyanobacteria multiplied, they made more and more oxygen. (Today, our atmosphere is 20 percent oxygen. Cyanobacteria and algae make at least half of the oxygen on Earth. Plants make the rest.)

All of this new oxygen set off a climate disaster. It destroyed the methane gas that had been keeping Earth nice and warm. Temperatures all over Earth dropped to −58 degrees Fahrenheit. The oceans were covered with ice a mile deep. Most living things died off.

Some microbes found homes deep under the surface of Earth, far away from the poisonous oxygen gas. Some moved to the bottom of the icy ocean. Others adapted to oxygen and made carbon dioxide, another gas that helps warm Earth. Life bounced back.[4]

Over time, cyanobacteria made it possible for life to move from water to land. Some of the oxygen gas they made became ozone. Ozone is a form of oxygen that makes a layer high in our atmosphere. The ozone layer filters out harmful rays from the sun that can cause deadly damage to cells. Now, it was safe for life to move from the protection of the oceans and lakes. Soon there would be living things on the entire surface of Earth.

Earth's Climate

Incredible as it seems, microbes play a direct role in Earth's climate today. Carbon dioxide is one of the most abundant greenhouse gases. Along with methane and some other gases, it traps the sun's heat in our atmosphere, just like a greenhouse traps heat inside it. Without these naturally occurring gases, the average temperature of Earth would be about zero degrees Fahrenheit. Instead, it is about 57 degrees Fahrenheit. If the levels of greenhouse gases get too high, Earth will become too warm.

Cyanobacteria and algae living in the upper layers of the surface of the ocean use billions of tons of carbon dioxide from the atmosphere. Until recently in Earth's history, photosynthetic organisms were able to keep the levels of carbon dioxide in the atmosphere fairly stable.

However, the burning of fossil fuels such as coal, oil, and natural gas has greatly increased the levels of carbon dioxide in the atmosphere. With more carbon dioxide in the atmosphere trapping heat, the temperature of Earth's surface has risen by about one degree Fahrenheit in the past century. It has increased sharply in the past

Cyanobacteria in the ocean change carbon dioxide (CO_2) in the air into food that ocean animals eat. By pulling the CO_2 out of the air, the bacteria help keep this greenhouse gas at a normal level.

two decades. Most scientists agree that the increased levels of carbon dioxide and other greenhouse gases are directly linked to global warming.

Ocean algae and bacteria affect our climate in another way, too. You may be familiar with that salty sea smell of the ocean. Part of that odor comes from gases produced by algae and bacteria near the surface. One of these gases is dimethyl sulfide (DMS). When DMS is released into the atmosphere, it combines with oxygen to form tiny, sulfur-containing particles. Water droplets stick to these particles. Together, these droplets cause clouds to form.

As clouds increase over the ocean, they reflect some of the sun's radiation, sending it away from Earth. This cools the ocean below. But as clouds increase and the surface of the ocean cools, the growth of algae and bacteria slows down. Fewer algae and bacteria means that less DMS is made, which decreases the amount of cloud cover. Now, the surface of the ocean becomes warmer, and the numbers of bacteria and algae increase. In this never-ending cycle, ocean microbes play an important role in keeping Earth's cloud cover "just right."[5]

These single-celled protozoans are called dinoflagellates. They live in saltwater. These protozoans have hollow "horns" that help them float in the water (x430).

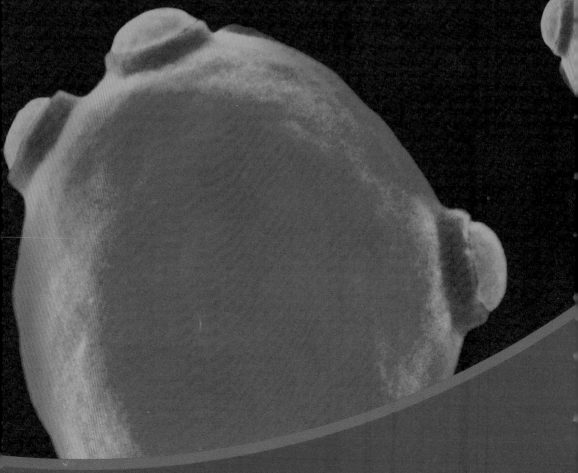

CHAPTER 4
Microbes at Work

What do penicillin and pizza have in common? Both are made with the help of microbes! Even before people knew that microbes existed, they used bacteria and yeast to help them make food and other useful products. In the past century, scientists have discovered new ways to put microbes to use making medicine and antibiotics, cleaning up toxic waste and landfills, identifying criminals, and much, much more.

Bread and Chocolate— Brought to You by Microbes

Flat breads, made from a mixture of pounded grains and water (similar to today's tortillas or matzo), probably date back to the Stone Age.

We don't know how or when someone discovered how to make raised bread, but we do know that archaeologists have uncovered signs that Egyptians were baking bread more than 4,000 years ago. Egyptian hieroglyphs also contain references to bread. The best guess is that some baker got distracted or delayed and let a bowl of flour and water sit longer than usual. The baker may have noticed that the flour and water mixture expanded and had an unusual smell. Not wanting to waste the flour and water, the baker probably shrugged and cooked the mixture anyway. Imagine the baker's delight when the result was lighter and tastier than the usual flat, hard bread![1]

What that baker could not have known was that yeast living on the grains and in the air began to grow and multiply in the flour and water mixture. As the yeast cells use the starches in the flour, they give off carbon dioxide gas and a small amount of alcohol. This process is called fermentation. The gas causes proteins (gluten) in the flour to stretch. The alcohol burns off as the bread bakes. Today many bakers simply use packaged yeast to make bread.

The ancient Egyptians also fermented grape juice to make wine, and grains to make beer. But they were not alone in "discovering" fermentation. For thousands of years, people all over the world have used fermenting yeast and bacteria to make and preserve foods. For example, fermenting bacteria make an acid that helps change cabbage into sauerkraut and cucumbers into pickles. Fermentation is the

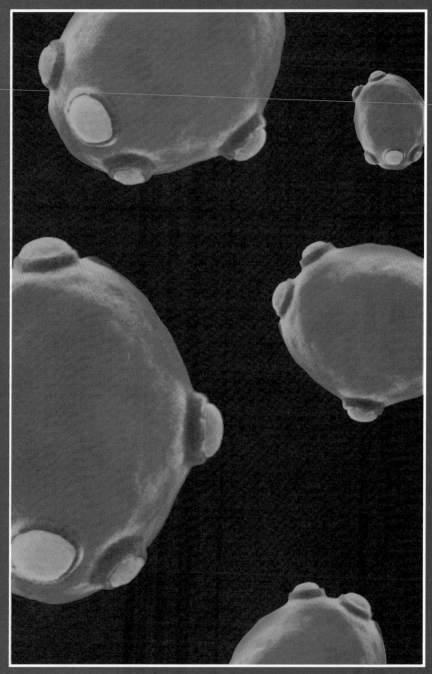

The yeast in bread dough is a microbe. These microbes give off carbon dioxide, which causes the dough to rise (x4,630–12,340).

first step in making coffee and chocolate. Lactic acid bacteria ferment milk
to make cheese, yogurt, buttermilk,
and sour cream.

Other bacteria and molds are often
added to cheese cultures. They make
chemicals that add flavor to the
cheese. Have you ever wondered why
there are holes in Swiss cheese? They come
from bubbles of carbon dioxide gas made by a
type of bacterium added to the cheese mixture.
The veins and strong taste of bleu cheese are
made by a mold injected into the cheese.

Other fermenting bacteria make a kind of
sugar commonly used to make ice cream and
chewing gum.

Penicillin and Other "Wonder Drugs"

At the start of the twentieth century, many people died from infections that are easily cured today. Because there were no antibiotics, an infected scratch could easily be deadly. In 1928, a Scottish microbiologist named Alexander Fleming was searching for substances that would kill disease-causing bacteria. Not the neatest or most organized scientist, he was straightening up a jumbled pile of petri dishes he had been using to grow bacteria. One of the

Alexander Fleming grew *Penicillium* bacterium in a petri dish in 1928.

dishes had become contaminated with some mold. Oddly enough, the bacteria that had been growing around the mold had all died. The mold, later identified as *Penicillium notatum*, made an antibiotic called penicillin.

A few years later, biochemist Ernst Chain and physician Howard Florey, working in England, recognized the importance of Fleming's discovery and began to study penicillin. They showed that it could be used to treat severe bacterial infections. By this time it was 1941, and Britain was at war. At that time, soldiers were more likely to die from infections following wounds than from the wounds themselves. Chain and Florey knew they could save thousands of lives if only they could make enough penicillin to treat the soldiers. Working with American scientists at a research center in Peoria, Illinois, they developed a way of mass-producing penicillin through fermentation techniques.[2] By the end of World War II, penicillin was available in large amounts for both military and civilian use.

The phenomenal success of penicillin led to the search for other antibiotic-producing organisms. Now there are many different antibiotics produced by a variety of molds or bacteria, each one specialized in treating different types of bacterial infections. Infectious diseases are no longer the leading cause of death. But now we have a new problem to worry about: antibiotic resistance. Antibiotics have become so widely used—in livestock feed, on fruit trees, and in treating human disease (even though only an estimated one-half of all antibiotics given to people are actually needed[3])—that some bacteria are developing resistance to the drugs.

High-Tech Microbes: The Birth of Modern Biotechnology

Unlike humans and other animals, bacteria do not need to have sex to reproduce. One cell just makes a copy of its genome and splits into two. But many bacteria do exchange pieces of DNA with other bacteria. One of the ways they do this is by swapping ring-shaped pieces of DNA called **plasmids**.

In the early 1970s, scientists discovered a clever use for the bacteria's habit of swapping plasmids. They realized that they could insert a gene into a plasmid that would be taken up by a bacterium. This process is called genetic engineering. As these bacteria reproduce, they make identical copies of themselves—and the new gene. Because bacteria multiply and grow so rapidly, scientists use these microbes to make huge numbers of any gene of interest. This is known as DNA cloning.

The first commercial use of genetic engineering was human insulin made by bacteria. People with diabetes must inject themselves with insulin, a hormone that regulates blood sugar levels. In the past, insulin was purified from pigs or other animals. It was expensive, and some people had bad reactions to the animal insulin. In 1978, a scientist named Herbert Boyer made a version of a human DNA insulin gene, spliced it into the bacterium *Escherichia coli* (*E. coli*), and grew the bacteria in the lab. Voila! As long as he could keep the bacteria growing and happy, he had a ready-made insulin factory.

Genetically engineered microbes have since been used to produce improved antibiotics and other useful human proteins. These include interferon (used to treat some forms of cancer and other diseases) and human growth hormone. Hepatitis A and B **vaccines** made from genetically engineered yeast cells have been approved for use in the United States. By the end of the year 2000, there were 84 "biotech medicines" approved for use in North America and Europe, benefiting about 250 million people.[4]

Genetic engineering is also widely used in plants used for food. You may have heard of the debate surrounding genetically modified (GM) foods. Many people worry that growing these plants could cause damage to the environment or that the foods themselves could be harmful to human health. Yet many scientists are convinced that genetic engineering can be safely used to make crops that are more nutritious or able to withstand disease. Some scientists are even experimenting with ways to put vaccines into plants. Someday, you may be able to eat a vaccine-carrying banana instead of getting a shot!

In 1985, scientists discovered a faster, simpler, and less expensive way of cloning DNA. This technique uses an enzyme isolated from a bacterium, *Thermus aquaticus*. It is called the polymerase chain reaction. (PCR).[5]

PCR techniques are now in widespread use, from diagnosing disease to solving crimes. Because it can rapidly multiply tiny amounts of DNA into quantities that scientists can more easily study, it can detect infections in their early stages. Using tiny biological samples (such as hair, saliva, sweat, or blood), forensic scientists can use PCR techniques to link a criminal to the scene of a crime. This is called DNA fingerprinting.

Genetic engineering is being used to make crops that are resistant to disease.

Real-life Jurassic Park

In the movie *Jurassic Park*, the scientists found fossilized, blood-sucking insects that had bitten living dinosaurs and then had been trapped in amber. The scientists used the DNA from the fossil blood to recreate dinosaurs. Although *Jurassic Park* was science fiction, there is a real-life version of the movie. In this version, scientists bring a deadly virus, not a dinosaur, back to life.

In 1918, a worldwide influenza (flu) epidemic killed between 20 and 40 million people. Perhaps the most deadly plague in human history, this epidemic was caused by an especially nasty strain of the flu virus. By the spring of 1919, the virus had disappeared as mysteriously as it appeared.

Fast-forward to the mid 1990s. A scientist named Jeffery Taubenberger wanted to know what made the 1918 influenza virus so deadly. He and other scientists hoped

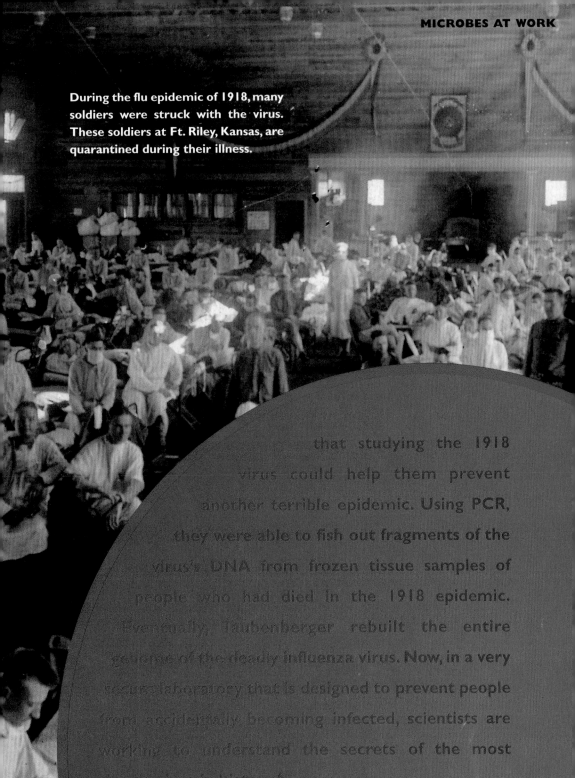

During the flu epidemic of 1918, many soldiers were struck with the virus. These soldiers at Ft. Riley, Kansas, are quarantined during their illness.

that studying the 1918 virus could help them prevent another terrible epidemic. Using PCR, they were able to fish out fragments of the virus's DNA from frozen tissue samples of people who had died in the 1918 epidemic. Eventually, Taubenberger rebuilt the entire genome of the deadly influenza virus. Now, in a very secure laboratory that is designed to prevent people from accidentally becoming infected, scientists are working to understand the secrets of the most deadly virus in history.[6]

Hardhat Area

Given enough time, microbes can break down just about any substance, returning potato peels to the soil, turning iron to rust, and changing dead fish into nitrogen-rich fertilizer. But they do it slowly, and ever-growing landfills and toxic spills require faster action. Scientists are learning to speed up the decay process, using microbes to break down hazardous pollutants into less toxic substances.

In the early 1950s, the U.S. government built a facility near the Savannah River in Georgia to produce materials for nuclear weapons. Two highly toxic liquids, sometimes called TCE, were used. Workers poured the TCE into underground tanks through pipes. Unfortunately, the pipes were leaky. The TCE seeped through the soil and into the underground water supplies that fed nearby wells and springs. Eventually, the TCE made its way into the food chain.

Scientist Terry Hazen found that methane-eating bacteria already living in the soil could break down the TCE—but very slowly. The scientists pumped methane and oxygen into the soil to increase the numbers of the methane-eating bacteria already living there. As the scientists decreased the methane levels, the ever-hungry methane-eating bacteria began to eat up TCE. Within a few months, the level of TCE in the soil was so low that scientists could no longer detect it.[7]

Microbes have become useful in the mining industry as well. Traditionally, ores were dug from the earth and crushed. Then heat or toxic chemicals were used to extract minerals such as copper or gold. This is an expensive process and bad for the environment. In the past few decades, the mining industry has begun to use microbes to

Oil collected on marsh plants.

extract the minerals instead. Given the proper nutrients, for example, a bacterium called *Thiobacillus ferroxidans* can chemically change rock to release copper. Scientists are now trying to find (or genetically engineer) other bacteria that can survive the high temperatures and toxic chemicals used in mining.[8]

Microbes can also clean up crude oil spills from ocean-going tankers, pesticide runoff from rivers, and polluted wastewater *before* it is released into the environment. Scientists have been using microbes to treat wastewater for over 100 years. Wastewater is the water that carries

wastes from homes, businesses, and industries. It contains sewage and other disgusting stuff. Treating wastewater is expensive, but it is necessary to prevent the spread of human disease and the pollution

This oil tanker in Louisiana spilled crude oil into Timbalier Bay.

of our waterways. Researchers at Pennsylvania State University have recently developed a fuel cell that can make electricity from wastewater treatment.[9] A fuel cell is like a battery; it generates electricity from a chemical reaction. In this case, as the microbes digest the waste material in the sewage, they help produce a steady electric current. The scientists believe that this technology could someday lower the energy costs of treating waste.

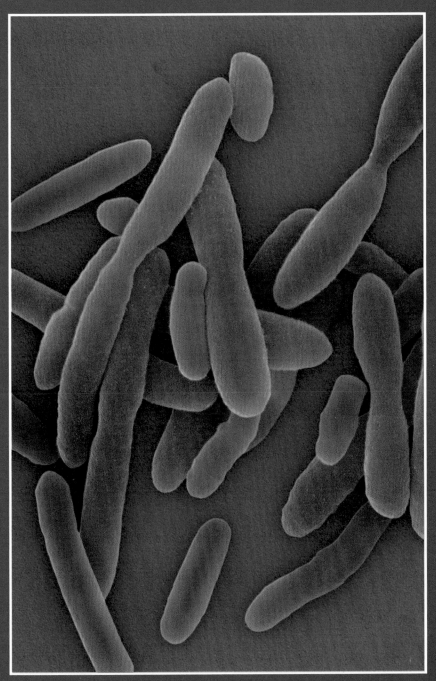

Pseudomonas bacteria are able to break down oil. Scientists use this microbe to help clean the environment (x14,060).

CHAPTER 5

Microbes, Disease, and Society

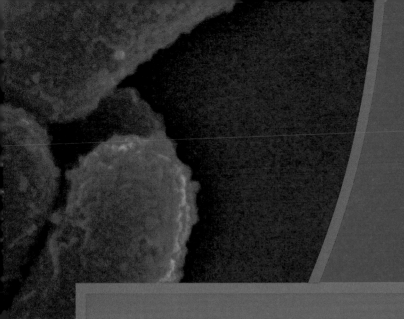

Ring around the rosie,
A pocket full of posies
Ashes, ashes,
We all fall down.

Some scholars and historians say that this old nursery rhyme is about the Black Death, the bubonic plague that struck

THE PLAGUE OF LONDON 1665.

Europe from 1347 to 1351. Around 20 million people—greater than one-third of Europe's population—died in this epidemic. The disease was caused by a bacterium called *Yersinia pestis*. The bacterium came to Europe in the gut of a flea, most likely one hitching a ride on a rat carried into an Italian shipping port. It would have been easy for infected fleas to jump from rats to sailors or townspeople. The biting fleas transferred Y. *pestis* to their unsuspecting victims, who in turn spread the bacterium when they sneezed or coughed.

One of the early signs of the disease is rose-colored rings on the skin. People carried posies, or flowers, to cover up the stench of illness and death. People who died of the disease were often cremated, which led to the reference to ashes. (Some versions say, "A-tishoo! A-tishoo," which mimics the sound of sneezing— a common symptom of the disease.) When the victims die, they "all fall down."[1]

Medieval medicine was powerless against the disease. Most Christians believed that they were being punished for their sins. In Germany and Switzerland, a group of people who called themselves Flagellants beat themselves with leather whips as punishment for their sins. They began to start rumors that the Jews were deliberately spreading the plague by polluting community wells, even though Jewish communities were equally affected by the plague. Thousands of Jews were killed. Many of those who survived fled to Poland, eastern Germany, Austria, and parts of Russia. This is why there were such large Jewish populations in those areas in the nineteenth and early twentieth centuries. Their descendents would be the targets of persecution and mass killings in Russia and Germany.[2]

Scholars believe that the labor shortages brought about by the Black Death helped end the feudal system, the major form of government in medieval Europe. Under the feudal system, lords or nobles pledged their loyalty to the king but managed their own lands much as they wished. Peasants worked for the lords, usually for very little money. After the Black Death, the few surviving peasants were much in demand. Many ran away from their lords to seek better jobs, either to other estates paying better wages or to cities to learn a trade. The nobles and lords became less powerful. Peasants began to demand, and received, better treatment.

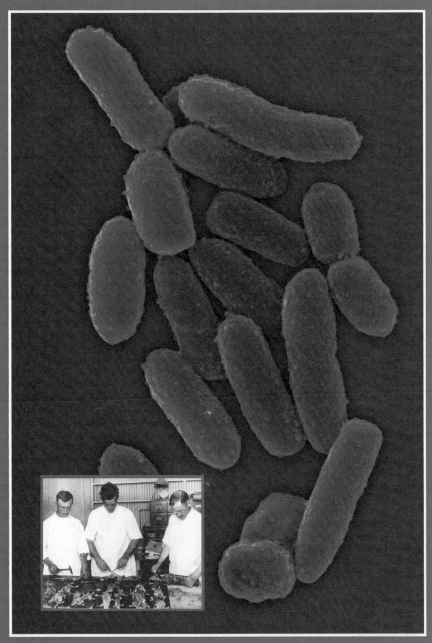

A 1914 photo (inset) shows workers in New Orleans examining rats that they suspect carry the bubonic plague. *Yersinia pestis* is the microbe that caused this plague throughout history. It is passed from rat fleas to humans (x14,625).

The plague occasionally reappeared in Europe and elsewhere, including China, into the twentieth century. It was not until the development of antibiotics in the 1940s that the plague could be successfully treated.

This is the way in which one disease, the Black Death, has changed the course of history. Other microbial diseases, such as smallpox, have shaped human evolution, influenced our behavior, and even led to the destruction of entire civilizations.

Agriculture and Disease

Well before the time of the Black Death, early hunter-gatherers lived in small, isolated groups that moved around frequently. They became infected by disease-causing microbes from the soil or wild animals. But the kinds of epidemic diseases that would later sweep from person to person, such as the bubonic plague, were probably very rare in these small, scattered societies.

As some of the hunter-gatherers began to settle down into a farming lifestyle, towns and cities began to grow. People lived in more crowded and less sanitary conditions than ever before, making it easier for disease-causing microbes to spread from one person to another. Many of the disease-causing microbes that cause us problems today came from domestic animals such as cows, sheep, pigs, and poultry. Early farmers lived in close contact with their livestock, and microbes must have passed freely between people and animals. The measles virus, for example, probably evolved from a virus that infects cattle.[3]

Infectious diseases caused by microbes that originally came from animals—such as smallpox, measles, influenza, typhus, and tuberculosis—swept through cities and towns. Many people died, but those who survived developed an immunity that protected them against the diseases. People who were able to fight off the disease lived to have children who were also better adapted at fighting these infections.

People living in the New World, such as the Aztecs in Mexico or the Mandan Indians of North America, also lived in large settlements or cities. However, there was one important difference between their way of life and that of the Europeans. Very few New World civilizations kept domesticated animals except perhaps dogs. These people were not exposed to disease-causing microbes from animals as frequently, and so they never developed resistance to those diseases.

In the sixteenth century, Spanish conquerors unwittingly brought smallpox to the New World. Many Aztecs in Mexico and Incans in Peru who were not killed by the Spanish armies fell to the disease and died from the resulting epidemic.

Spanish conquerors infected people in the New World with smallpox. The disease killed many Aztecs and Incas.

Spaniards and European explorers brought smallpox and other diseases to large North American tribes as well, with terrible results. According to Jared Diamond, an author and professor of physiology at the University of California Los Angeles, "For the New World as a whole, the Indian population decline in the century or two following Columbus's arrival is estimated to have been as large as 95 percent. The main killers were Old World germs to which Indians had never been exposed…"[4]

The first introduction of smallpox and other devastating infectious diseases to the New World was an accident. Later, during the French and Indian War, however, the British intentionally smuggled blankets that had been infected with the smallpox virus to unsuspecting Indians. The disease took a heavy toll on the native peoples. This is one of the first documented examples of biological warfare.[5]

Napoleon's Most Deadly Enemies

In the summer of 1812, the French emperor Napoleon Bonaparte assembled an army of about 265,000 men to invade Russia. With additional soldiers from Germany and Austria, Napoleon commanded over 600,000 troops. It should have been a slam-dunk for Napoleon, who expected an easy win because his army greatly outnumbered the Russian forces. But the long march through Poland took a huge toll on his soldiers. Food supplies ran low, water supplies were polluted with disease-causing microbes, and the troops began to suffer from malnutrition and dysentery (serious diarrhea caused by an amoeba).

As the troops crossed into Russia, some of the soldiers began to develop a high fever and rash, the first symptoms of typhus. Typhus is a disease caused by a bacterium called *Rickettsia prowazekii*. These bacteria are often carried by lice, a common pest in filthy conditions like those the soldiers endured in their long march to Russia. Many of the soldiers infected with the organism died quickly. Those who did not die were often too sick to fight.

Although the half-starved, sick soldiers struggled on to Moscow, they were eventually forced to retreat. By that time, winter had begun, and the weather was intensely cold.

Many more men died of typhus, pneumonia, and dysentery. By the time Napoleon's once-splendid army retreated, fewer than 40,000 soldiers remained. A tiny fraction of those were ever again fit for duty.[6] Although Napoleon continued to fight battles in Europe, his defeat in Russia marked the beginning of the end of his rule.

Napoleon and his army invaded Russia in 1812. Many of his men died of typhus, caused by the bacterium *Rickettsia prowazekii*.

Irish Potato Famine

In the nineteenth century, all of Ireland was under British rule. Most of the land was owned by wealthy English and Protestant Irish, who divided their estates up into small plots of land they rented to Irish Catholic farmers. The tenant farmers and laborers who worked for them had a hard life. Their main food was the potato. Potatoes were cheap and plentiful. They supplied almost all the nutrients of a healthy diet when combined with milk. What little grain was grown in Ireland was exported to the English market. Britain's harsh policies toward

The potato was the main food of Ireland. When the fungus *Phytophthora* caused disease in the crop, almost half of the potatoes in Ireland rotted.

Ireland left its peasants dependent on one staple food, the potato.

In 1845, the leaves on potato plants suddenly turned black, curled, and rotted. They gave off a terrible smell. Potatoes dug out of the ground rotted within days. A microscopic, airborne fungus called *Phytophthora infestans* caused the blight. The fungus, which had been transported in the holds of ships traveling from North America to England, was carried by the wind to the countryside of Ireland. *P. infestans* settled on the leaves of healthy plants, multiplied, and spread to surrounding plants. A single infected potato plant could infect thousand of other plants in just a few days.[7]

The potato blight destroyed 40 percent of that year's crop, and nearly 100 percent the next year. By 1851, 1.5 million Irish people had died of starvation or of diseases related to the famine. Another million people emigrated, many of them to North America or Australia. Among the Irish families seeking new lives in the United States were the Fitzgeralds and the Kennedys. These families were ancestors of John F. Kennedy, the first Irish Catholic president of the United States.

A Protozoan, a Mosquito, and Human Evolution

Malaria is a disease that affects 300 to 500 million people each year. It is caused by a protozoan called *Plasmodium falciparum*, which infects red blood cells. It is transmitted to people by the bite of an infected mosquito.[8] This protozoan evolved in Africa around 3,200 to 7,000 years ago, around the time that people began clearing rainforests for agriculture. The clearings created more sunlit pools where mosquitoes like to breed.[9]

Over time, some of the people living in that area developed a genetic **mutation** (change) that caused their red blood cells to warp into a sickle shape, especially when the people were active. Those who had two copies of the mutated gene developed sickle cell anemia, a severe and usually fatal disease in primitive populations. But those who inherited only one copy of the sickle cell gene had no symptoms in ordinary conditions. They were also more resistant

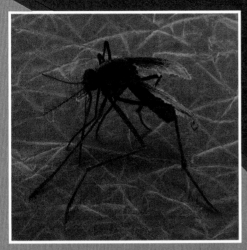

(x15)

to malaria than people who didn't have the mutation. When their red blood cells became infected with the protozoan, they turned into the sickle shape. An organ called the spleen destroys these sickle-shaped red blood cells, along with the microbe.

People with one sickle cell gene were more likely to survive a malaria infection and pass on the protective gene to their own children. Today, we can see that sickle cell anemia is especially common among people whose ancestors came from certain parts of Africa.

91

AIDS:
The Current Plague

Sadly, epidemic diseases are far from being a thing of the past. We are in the midst of an AIDS (Acquired Immunodeficiency Syndrome) epidemic, caused by a virus called HIV (Human Immunodeficiency Virus). The epidemic spans the entire globe. Since the first case of AIDS was diagnosed in 1981, more than 20 million people have died of AIDS, and around 40 million people are currently living with the AIDS virus. Over 3 million died of AIDS in 2004 alone.[10] The virus is spread by sexual contact with an infected person, by sharing needles or syringes with someone who is infected, or (rarely) through blood transfusions. Babies born to HIV-infected mothers may become infected before or during birth, or through breast-feeding.

Although AIDS in the United States was initially seen primarily in gay men and injection drug users, that is no longer the case. Globally, nearly half of all people infected with the virus between the ages of 15 and 49 are women. In Africa, nearly 60 percent of HIV-positive persons are women. Women are not only more physically susceptible to infection than men, but in many traditional societies women have little power to insist that their male partners practice safe sex. Because women are often the primary caregivers, they end up shouldering much of the burden of taking care of sick family members.

Hardest hit by the epidemic are poor countries, especially those in Africa. Just under two-thirds of all people living with HIV are in sub-Saharan Africa.[11] The epidemic is tearing apart the societies of hard-hit countries. In Zimbabwe, the average life expectancy has dropped from 70 to 38 years. By 2010, it is estimated that there will be 20 million African children who are orphans because their parents have died of AIDS. They will most likely grow up in terrible poverty and without adult care. Economies suffer, as more and more people are no longer able to work. Famines and food shortages are made even worse by AIDS-affected families no longer able to plant their own crops.

In addition, AIDS makes people more susceptible to other infectious diseases, including tuberculosis. Tuberculosis (TB), which is caused

A lab technician that works for the Centers for Disease Control and Prevention (CDC) does research on the AIDS virus.

by the bacterium *Mycobacterium tuberculosis,* is spread through the air like the common cold. TB is one of the oldest known diseases. Egyptian mummies and paintings show that TB was common at least 4,000 years ago. It has been a major killer over the centuries. With the development of effective antibiotics in the 1940s, many doctors predicted an end to tuberculosis epidemics. But since the 1980s, new, more dangerous strains of the bacterium, resistant to antibiotics, have arisen. The World Health Organization estimates that TB caused 1.75 million deaths in 2003—most of them in Africa and other poor countries.[12]

AIDS can be prevented through education about the ways in which HIV is transmitted and by giving people ways to protect themselves. There are now effective drugs that allow HIV-positive people to live longer, more productive lives. But these steps require money, something many desperately poor countries lack. Analysts say that a worldwide effort is needed to stop the AIDS epidemic.

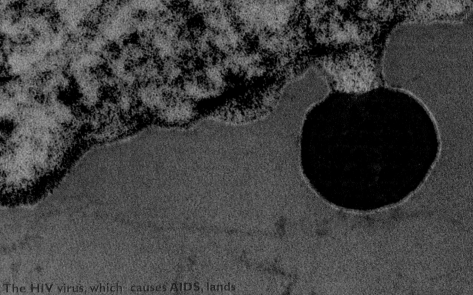

The HIV virus, which causes AIDS, lands on human cells. Viruses need other cells in order to make copies of themselves (x262,485).

CHAPTER 6

Is Anybody Out There?

When Italian astronomer Giovanni Schiaparelli made a map of Mars in 1877, he showed a system of what he called *canali*—the Italian word for channels. The word was mistakenly translated into English as "canals," and many people were convinced that this was evidence that intelligent Martians had built waterways to transport water from the polar ice caps of Mars to the drier parts of the planet. Since that time, Mars has been considered the most likely of the other planets in our solar system to harbor life.

In his 1898 science fiction book *The War of the Worlds*, H.G. Wells imagined that invading Martians looked something like squid with enormous eyes. But if there is life on Mars, or other planets for that matter, it is more likely to resemble a microbe.

Scientists continue to debate the likelihood that there is intelligent life elsewhere in the universe. But many agree that microbial life could be common. Microbes from other planets are unlikely to land on Earth in microscopic spaceships, although it is possible that they have arrived on meteorites. Nor will they send out tiny radio signals to alert us to their presence. Therefore, scientists are developing technologies to detect life on other planets. **Astrobiology** is the rapidly growing science devoted to the study of life in the universe—how it began, where it exists now, and what the future might bring.

In 1975, the National Aeronautics and Space Administration (NASA) sent two Viking probes to Mars, considered the planet most likely to contain life. When the Viking probes landed on Mars in 1976, they found only a barren, frozen landscape. Scientists who studied the soil found no building blocks of living things. In fact, it seemed to contain chemicals that would destroy living cells.[1] It seemed clear that Mars, the Red Planet, was a dead planet. The search for life on Mars, not to mention other planets, seemed to have reached a dead end.

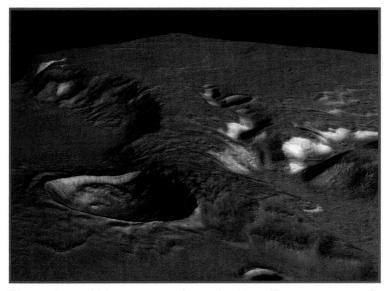

The surface of Mars, as seen from the Mars Express spacecraft, has low areas and high areas that look like channels. This region is between two centers of volcanic activity.

Extreme Life— On Earth

It took some amazing discoveries here on Earth to make scientists rethink the possibility of life on other planets. In the late 1970s, oceanographers from the Woods Hole Oceanographic Institute crammed themselves into a tiny submersible vessel called *Alvin*. They explored an underwater mountain range near the Galápagos Islands. There, they found superheated water the color of smoke spewing from volcanic vents, often surrounded by a chimney of rock. The temperature of the water gushing from the vents was 350 degrees Celsius. That is more than three times the temperature of boiling water at sea level! (The immense pressure at the bottom of the ocean prevents the water from boiling.)

Even so, the area surrounding the vents was teeming with life, including those tubeworms and their symbiotic bacteria described in Chapter 2. The scientists found microbes living inside the chimneys, where temperatures were a blistering 110 degrees Celsius! Scientists had never imagined life could survive at such high temperatures.

Even more surprising was the fact that all of this life seemed to thrive without the benefit of the sun's energy. Biologists had long thought that every food chain depended, directly or indirectly, on photosynthesis. But there is no sunlight at 3,000 meters under the surface of the ocean. This food chain was different. At the bottom of this food chain were heat-loving microbes. Instead of using the sun's energy, they use the chemicals spewing from the vents.[2]

Since then, scientists have found microbes living in other weird places: in sheets of ice in the Arctic and Antarctic and in rocks a mile below the surface of Earth. Microbes live in acid strong enough to burn your skin, and in nuclear waste. In short, if you can dish it out, there will be some kind of microbe that can take it. All they need are the building blocks of life (carbon, hydrogen, oxygen, nitrogen, and a few other elements), some

A black smoker vent several miles below the surface of the Atlantic Ocean gives off dark, mineral-rich water. The temperature of this water is hundreds of degrees Celsius. Deep sea vents provide an unusual habitat to some forms of bacteria and deep sea crabs.

sort of energy source, and liquid water. Maybe the idea of finding life on other planets wasn't so far-fetched after all! The question was, How would scientists find it? How would they even know what to look for?

To answer those questions, scientists are developing methods of testing for life on Earth that can be used to explore similar environments on Mars. For example, the Atacama Desert in Chile is so dry that NASA uses it as a model for Mars. The driest parts of the desert get virtually no rain; the "wet" parts get about half an inch every year. The barren landscape

looks completely lifeless. Until 2003, scientists believed that the driest parts of the desert were sterile (without life).

After much searching, however, researchers found traces of life on some of the rocks they had gathered from the Atacama Desert. Later, back in the lab, they were able to cultivate bacteria from those rocks. Other scientists have found bacteria by digging a foot below the desert's surface.

In October 2005, a team of scientists interested in the search for life on other planets made an exciting announcement. Inside an

The Atacama Desert in Chile is one of the driest places on Earth. Researchers use the desert as a model of Mars when looking for life in extreme environments.

extinct frozen volcano, they had found a complex and rare community of microbes. Some were living and some were fossilized. These microbes, found inside the ice itself and on the surfaces and cracks of volcanic rocks, were adapted to live in extremely cold conditions. This amazing discovery was made not on Mars but on a remote island north of the Arctic Circle.

"Ice-filled volcanic vents, such as these, are likely to occur on Mars and may be a potential habitat for life there," explained one of the scientists, Andrew Steele of the Carnegie Institution's Geophysical Laboratory.[3]

Microbes that live within caves could also provide clues about what life under the surface of Mars might be like. We know that Mars had huge volcanoes that might have created caves, perhaps much like those on Earth. A group of scientists called the SLIME (Subsurface Life in Mineral Environments) team studies microorganisms in a cave in southern Mexico called Cueva de Villa Luz. Inside this cave, there are high levels of hydrogen sulfide gas (it smells like rotten eggs). Hydrogen sulfide can be extremely poisonous to humans, so the scientists must wear gas masks inside the cave. The hydrogen sulfide combines with oxygen to produce sulfuric acid—as strong as battery acid—that eats away at the limestone and burns holes in the scientists' clothing. [4]

The microbes grow in underground streams in slippery clumps the scientists call "phlegm balls." They hang from the ceiling in gooey, stalactite-like drips called "snottites," and they carpet the floor of the cave in a green slimy layer. The microbes make the slime, called a biofilm, because it gives them a surface to grow on and helps protect them from the sulfuric acid. Amazingly, spiders, insects, fish, and even bats also make their home in this cave. One of the scientists on the SLIME team, Penelope Boston, says that environments like this can teach us a lot about life's limits. When we look for life on other worlds, "it may be that we will find a whole planet where all the inhabitants arose and evolved under conditions similar to an extreme Earth environment. They will hardly be 'extremophiles,' but rather garden-variety specimens on their planet and not extreme at all!"[5]

Recipe for Life

A basic cookie recipe typically calls for flour, butter, sugar, and eggs. You might add chocolate chips, oatmeal, nuts, or flavoring such as vanilla or almond extract, but the basic ingredients are the same. Once the ingredients are assembled, you bake them in an oven. The dough can be dropped onto a cookie sheet or rolled out and cut into shapes. Chocolate chip cookies, gingerbread men, oatmeal, sugar, and peanut butter cookies—they look and taste different, but they're all cookies.

You can think of living things in a similar way: Humans may not look much like bacteria, but as living things we have some of the same basic requirements. We need the same building blocks: carbon, hydrogen, oxygen, nitrogen, and phosphorus. We need water. We need a source of energy—from

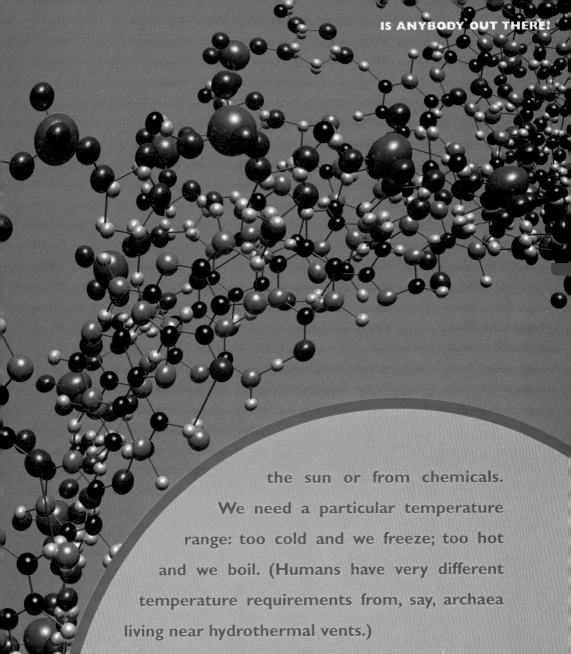

the sun or from chemicals. We need a particular temperature range: too cold and we freeze; too hot and we boil. (Humans have very different temperature requirements from, say, archaea living near hydrothermal vents.)

The search for life on other planets, then, begins with the search for the ingredients and requirements of living things: basic building blocks, water (or other liquid), an energy source, and a tolerable temperature range.

Follow the Water

Scientists looking for signs of life on Mars "follow the water," according to astrobiologist Jack Farmer of Arizona State University. "[Water] is considered one of the most fundamental requirements for living systems."[6] Any water on the surface of Mars would have evaporated into space when the planet began to lose its atmosphere, perhaps 3.8 billion years ago. Even so, scientists have found signs of water in the past. There may still be water deep under the surface of the planet.

In 2004, two robots the size of golf carts landed on the surface of Mars. Their primary mission: to search for signs of life—especially water. The robots were guided by remote control by a team of drivers at the Jet Propulsion Lab in California. These robots chugged up and down hills and tooled around craters, sending pictures and other data back to Earth. They found convincing evidence that there once was water on the surface of Mars—lots of it, either a large lake or shallow sea. The minerals they found in the waterbed showed that the water was probably salty.

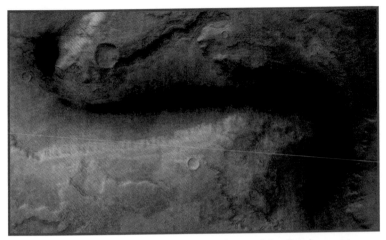

Channel on the surface of Mars once formed by flowing water.

The European Space Agency's *Mars Express* spacecraft, which has been orbiting Mars since 2003, sent back images of a frozen sea under the surface of the planet, glaciers, and a volcano that may have been active fairly recently.[7] In 2004, *Mars Express* detected the presence of ammonia and methane in the atmosphere of Mars. This was stunning news for astrobiologists. Both of these gases break down over time when they are exposed to sunlight. That means that something under the surface of the planet is constantly producing the gases. From what we know here on Earth, there are only two explanations for the methane and ammonia. They come either from active volcanoes or from living things.

An artist's painting of the *Mars Express* spacecraft as it approaches Mars. The spacecraft reached Mars in 2003 and has been sending photos of the surface of the planet back to Earth.

Microbes on the Moons?

We know that our moon does not harbor life, but astrobiologists believe that conditions might be right for living things on other moons in our solar system.

Scientists have found that Europa, one of Jupiter's moons, most likely has a cold, salty ocean beneath its frozen, icy surface. Spacecraft launched in the late 1970s made some detailed observations of Europa and her sister moons, Io, Callisto, and Ganymede. Images of Europa sent back to Earth show icy plates that have been broken apart and shifted into new positions, like icebergs in the Arctic Ocean. Scientists who study life in very cold temperatures have discovered organisms living in the water-filled cracks and fractures in Arctic ice. These cracks are likely to be present on Europa, too. The ocean under the ice crust is a promising place to search for life.

Researchers are also studying Saturn's moon, Titan, for signs of life. If life does exist on Titan, it would be very different from life on Europa. In January 2005, a spacecraft launched by the

European Space Agency landed on the surface of Titan. The spacecraft, called Huygens, survived only three hours in Titan's brutal cold (-291 degrees Fahrenheit), but in those three hours it sent pictures and data back to Earth.

Titan has a hazy atmosphere made mostly of nitrogen. It also has methane, hydrogen, and other compounds. Huygens landed on a

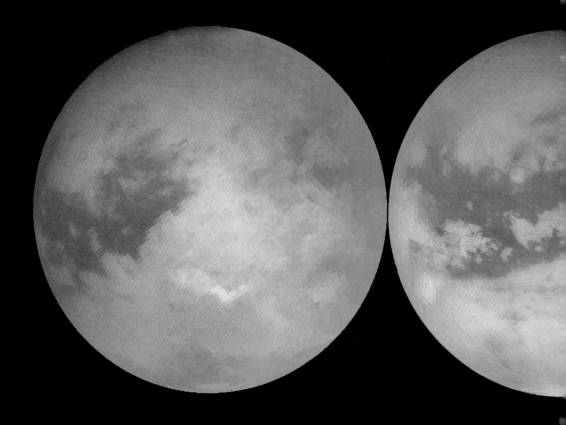

Titan is one of the moons of Saturn. These three photos were taken of the moon at different times, showing the different features of this moon. Scientists study Titan for signs of life.

dry streambed that was probably made by liquid methane. On the ground, there are rocks of ice as hard as granite. Nearby are channels that might be filled with liquid methane that rains down from the atmosphere. There are also signs of underground springs of liquid methane, although scientists have recently found that microbes do not make the gas.[8]

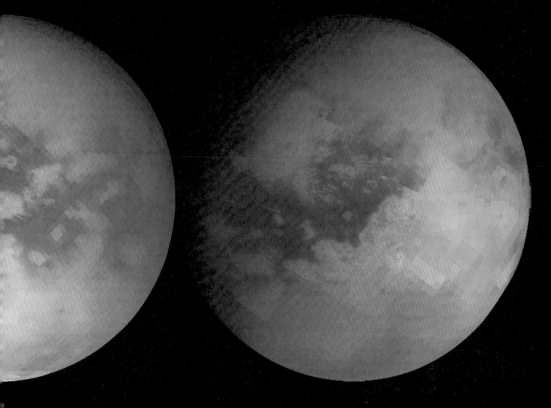

"It's Life, Captain, But Not Life as We Know It."

Earthlings are known as carbon-based life because this very common element is a major building block of living things. But is this the only way to make life? Another element, silicon, shares many chemical properties with carbon. (Silicon is the main component of many rocks on Earth.) Like carbon, there is lots of it in our galaxy. Both elements can combine with four hydrogen atoms. Silicon atoms don't form chains or rings very well, though. Chains and rings are important to carbon-based life. Still, some scientists have shown (at least on paper) that silicon life may be possible at very cold or very hot temperatures.

Water is also essential to Earth life. It is necessary for all of the chemical reactions that take place in living things. However, it is possible to imagine a form of life that depends on a liquid other than water. Life-forms on worlds that are much colder than Earth, such as Europa or Titan, might depend on compounds such as ammonia or methane that remain liquid at very low temperatures.

If life on other planets exists, perhaps, as Commander Spock said in *Star Trek: The Motion Picture*, "It's life, Captain, but not life as we know it."

The Good, the Bad, and the Slimy

Are we alone in the universe? That question remains to be answered. It does seem likely that we have microbial companions on other planets. Microbes can be found living in hydrothermal vents at the bottom of the ocean, embedded in Antarctic ice, in your gut, and floating in the clouds. Friend or foe, microbes are essential players in the game of life here on Earth—and perhaps elsewhere.

Chapter Notes

CHAPTER 1. Invisible World

1. Maya Pines, "The Friendly Bacteria Within Us," *Howard Hughes Medical Institute Bulletin*, Winter 2005, pp. 26, 28.

2. Samuel Hoole, trans., *The Select Works of Antony van Leeuwenhoek*, Vol. 1 (first printed 1798; reprint New York: Arno Press, 1977), p. 118.

3. Cynthia Needham, et. al., *Intimate Strangers: Unseen Life on Earth* (Washington, D.C.: ASM Press, 2000), p. 6.

4. Luis P. Villarreal, "Are Viruses Alive?" *Scientific American*, December 2004, pp. 101–105.

CHAPTER 2. We Are Not Alone

1. John Travis, "Gut Check: The Bacteria in Your Intestines Are Welcome Guests," *Science News Online*, <http://www.sciencenews.org/articles/20030531/bob9.asp.> From *Science News*, May 31, 2003, p. 344.

2. *Inventory of U.S. Greenhouse Gas Emissions and Sinks: 1990–2001*, U.S. Environmental Protection Agency, April 15, 2003.

3. Michael Gross, *Life on the Edge: Amazing Creatures Thriving in Extreme Environments* (New York: Plenum Press, 1998), p. 26.

4. Tom Wakeford, *Liaisons of Life: From Hornworts to Hippos, How the Unassuming Microbe Has Driven Evolution* (New York: John Wiley & Sons, Inc., 2001), pp. 21–26.

5. Visick, Karen L. and Margaret J. McFall-Ngai, "An Exclusive Contract: Specificity in the *Vibrio fischeri-Euprymna scolopes* Partnership," *Journal of Bacteriology*, April 2000, pp. 1779–1787.

6. Gross, p. 42.

CHAPTER 3. How Microbes Shape Our World

1. "Lichen Cosmonauts?" *Astrobiology Magazine*, November 12, 2005, <http://www.astrobio.net/news/modules.php?op=modload&name=News&file=article&sid=1771.

2. J. William Schopf, *Cradle of Life: The Discovery of Earth's Earliest Fossils* (Princeton, N.J.: Princeton University Press, 1999), p. 76.

3. James F. Kasting, "When Methane Made Climate," *Scientific American*, July 2004, pp. 80–85.

4. "Snowball Earth Culprit Found?" *Astrobiology Magazine*, August 7, 2005, <http://www.astrobio.net/news/article1671.html>.

5. Cynthia Needham, et. al., *Intimate Strangers: Unseen Life on Earth* (Washington, D.C.: American Society for Microbiology Press, 2000), pp. 34–35.

CHAPTER 4. Microbes at Work

1. Harold McGee, *On Food and Cooking: The Science and Lore of the Kitchen* (Fireside, New York: 1984), p. 275.

2. "The Top Pharmaceuticals That Changed the World," *Chemical and Engineering News*, June 20, 2005, <http://pubs.acs.org/cen/cover-story/83/8325/8325penicillin.html>.

3. Cynthia Needham, et. al., *Intimate Strangers: Unseen Life on Earth* (Washington, DC: ASM Press, 2000), p. 142.

4. Gary Walsh, "Biopharmaceutical Benchmarks–2003," *Nature Biotechnology*, November 2003, <http://www.nature.com/nbt/journal/v21/n8/full/nbt0803-865.html>.

5. Tabitha M. Powledge, "The Polymerase Chain Reaction," *Breakthroughs in Bioscience*, Federation of American Societies for Experimental Biology, <http://opa.faseb.org/pdf/The%20Polymerase%20Chain%20Reaction.pdf>.

6. Jamie Shreeve, "Why Revive a Deadly Flu Virus?" *The New York Times Magazine*, January 29, 2006, pp. 50–52.

7. Needham, et. al., pp. 151–153.

8. "Biomining," *NBIAP News Report*, U.S. Department of Agriculture, June 1994, <http://www.accessexcellence.org/RC/AB/BA/Biomining.html>.

9. Hong Liu, Ramanathan Ramnarayanan, and Bruce E. Logan, "Production of Electricity During Wastewater Treatment Using a Single Chamber Microbial Fuel Cell," *Environmental Science & Technology*, 2004, p. 2281.

CHAPTER 5. Microbes, Disease, and Society

1. Norman Cantor, *In the Wake of the Plague: The Black Death and the World It Made* (New York: The Free Press, 2001), pp. 5–6.

2. Philip Ziegler, *The Black Death* (Wolfeboro Falls, N.H.: Alan Sutton Publishing, Inc., 1991), pp. 62–80.

3. Jared Diamond, *Guns, Germs, and Steel: The Fates of Human Societies* (New York: W.W. Norton & Co., 1997), p. 206.

4. Ibid., p. 211.

5. G.W. Christopher, et. al., "Biological Warfare: A Historical Perspective," *Journal of the American Medical Association*, August 6, 1997, p. 412.

6. Frederick F. Cartwright, *Disease and History* (New York: Dorset Press, 1972), pp. 89–92, 97–102.

7. *The History Place: Irish Potato Famine, The Blight Begins*, <http://www.historyplace.com/worldhistory/famine/begins.htm>.

8. Pim Martens, and Lisbeth Hall, "Malaria on the Move: Human Population Movement and Malaria Transmission," *Emerging Infectious Diseases*, March–April 2000, pp. 103–109.

9. Jennifer C.C. Hume, Emily J. Lyons, and Karen P. Day, "Human Migration, Mosquitoes and the Evolution of *Plasmodium falciparum*," *Trends in Parasitology*, March 2003, pp. 144–149.

10. "AIDS Epidemic Update: 2004," Joint United Nations Programme on HIV/AIDS (UNAIDS), World Health Organization (WHO), Executive Summary I and II, <http://www.unaids.org/bangkok2004/report.html>.

11. Ibid.

12. "Tuberculosis: Infection and Transmission." Fact Sheet, World Health Organization, <http://www.who.int/mediacentre/factsheets/fs104/en/>.

CHAPTER 6. Is Anybody Out There?

1. Peter D. Ward, *Life as We Do Not Know It: The NASA Search for (and Synthesis of) Alien Life* (New York: Viking Penguin, 2005), p. 180.

2. Michael Gross, *Life on the Edge: Amazing Creatures Thriving in Extreme Environments* (New York: Plenum Press, 1998), pp. 22–26.

3. Michael Ray Taylor, *Dark Life: Martian Nanobacteria, Rock-eating Cave Bugs, and Other Extreme Organisms of Inner Earth and Outer Space,* (New York: Scribner, 1999), pp. 250–255.

4. Penelope Boston, "Life Below and Life 'Out There'," *GeoTimes*, August 2000, <http://www.agiweb.org/geotimes/aug00/lechuguilla.html>.

5. "Life in Ice," *Astrobiology Magazine*, October 5, 2005, <http://www.astrobio.net/news/modules.php?op=modload&name=News&file=article&sid=1737>.

6. "Deciphering Mars: Follow the Water," *Astrobiology Magazine*, September 12, 2005. <http://www.astrobio.net/news/modules.php?op=modload&name=News&file=article&sid=1709>.

7. Jenny Hogan, and Kelly Young, "Mars, Not Dead But Very Much Alive," *New Scientist*, Feb. 26, 2005, p. 10.

8. Leslie Mullen, "Titan: Passport to the Early Earth?" *Astrobiology Magazine,* December 1, 2005, <http://www.astrobio.net/news/modules.php?op=modload&name=News&file=article&sid=1790>.

Glossary

algae (AL-jee), plural of alga (AL-ga)—Protists that can carry out photosynthesis.

ammonia—A molecule made of one nitrogen atom and three hydrogen atoms.

antibiotic—A substance made by an organism (such as a fungus or bacterium) that inhibits or kills harmful microbes.

archaea (ar-KEY-uh)—Single-celled organisms that resemble bacteria. Like bacteria, their genome (DNA) is not enclosed in a cellular compartment called the nucleus. The makeup of their DNA, however, is more like that of eukaryotes. Many archaea thrive in some of the most hostile environments on Earth, and they are among the earliest forms of life on Earth.

asteroid—A small, rocky object that orbits a star.

astrobiology—A branch of biology concerned with the search for life on other planets.

bacteria, plural of bacterium—Members of a larger group of single-celled organisms. Their genome (DNA) is not enclosed in a cellular compartment called the nucleus. Bacteria come in many shapes, from rod-like to round to corkscrews, and they live in or on just about every person, place, or thing on Earth.

carbohydrate—A molecule made of carbon, hydrogen, and oxygen. Many carbohydrates are made by plants and are an important class of animal foods.

carbon dioxide—A molecule made of one carbon atom and two oxygen atoms.

colony—A mass of microbes growing together on a solid surface. There are so many of them that the colony can be seen with the naked eye.

cyanobacteria (sy-AN-oh-bak-TEER-ee-uh)—A type of bacteria that makes carbohydrates and oxygen from carbon dioxide in the air and water. It uses sunlight as a source of energy.

DNA—Stands for "deoxyribonucleic acid" (dee-OX-ee-RIBE-oh-new-CLAY-ick AS-id). DNA is the molecule that carries the genetic instructions in all forms of organisms except some viruses.

enzyme—A protein produced by living cells that can start or speed up reactions without itself being permanently altered.

epidemic—Disease that spreads widely and affects many individuals at one time.

eukaryote (YOU-carry-oat)—An organism made of one or more cells, with each cell having a separate nucleus. Plants, fungi, and animals are all eukaryotes.

evolution—The process by which the characteristics of organisms change over time.

fermentation—The chemical breakdown of a substance by microbes when oxygen is not present. It is often accompanied by the formation of gas.

fungi (FUN-jeye or FUN-guy)—Single-celled organisms that can live as individuals (like yeast) or in bunches (like mushrooms). Their genome, or DNA, is enclosed in a cellular compartment called the nucleus. Although some fungi resemble plants, they do not make their own food as plants do. Instead, they absorb nutrients from plant or animal matter.

genome (JEE-nome)—The hereditary information of an organism that is encoded in the DNA (or, for some viruses, in RNA).

greenhouse gas—Any one of the gases in the atmosphere that traps the sun's heat and warms Earth. Some greenhouse gases are naturally occurring; others result from human activity.

hydrothermal vent—A place on the ocean floor where hot, chemical-filled water flows up through cracks in Earth's crust.

immune system—Cells, tissues, and chemicals that the body uses to protect itself from foreign cells and substances.

lichen (LIE-ken)—A combination of fungi and green algae (and/or cyanobacteria) that live in a mutually beneficial relationship.

meteorite—A chunk of rock or metal from outer space that strikes the surface of Earth.

methane—A molecule containing one carbon atom and four hydrogen atoms.

microbe—An organism that can only be seen with the aid of a microscope. A microorganism.

molecule—A unit of two or more atoms. A molecule's atoms may be of the same or different elements.

mutation—A change in the genome. Mutations change the genetic information encoded in the genes.

nucleus—The separate compartment in eukaryotic cells that holds the genome.

organism—An individual living thing.

photosynthesis—The process by which plants and some bacteria make carbohydrates and oxygen from water and carbon dioxide in the air. The process stores energy from sunlight.

plasmid—A small circular portion of DNA separate from the main genome of a bacterium.

prokaryote (pro-CARRY-oat)—A one-celled organism that does not have a nucleus.

protist—A type of single-celled organism belonging to one of three major categories: the plantlike forms, or algae; the funguslike forms, like slime molds; and the animal-like forms, like protozoans (including amoebas). Their genetic material, or DNA, is enclosed in a cellular compartment called the nucleus. They are a type of eukaryote.

protozoan—A single-celled protist with some animal-like characteristics.

RNA—Ribonucleic acid. RNA is the molecule that helps turn the information encoded in genes into proteins. Some viruses carry their genetic information in RNA rather than DNA.

vaccine—A substance made from dead or weakened disease-causing microbes, or parts of them, that can cause a specific immune response against that microbe.

virus—Microscopic package of DNA or RNA in a protein coat. Viruses can multiply only by using the genome of living cells.

Further Reading

Bang, Molly. *Chattanooga Sludge*. New York: Harcourt-Brace & Co., 1996.

Dixon, Bernard. *Power Unseen: How Microbes Rule the World*. New York: W.H. Freeman & Co., 1994.

Giblin, James Cross. *When Plague Strikes: The Black Death, Smallpox, AIDS*. New York: HarperCollins Publishers, 1995.

Kramer, Stephen, and Dennis Kunkel. *Hidden Worlds: Looking Through a Scientist's Microscope*. Boston: Houghton-Mifflin, 2001.

Needham, Cynthia, et. al. *Intimate Strangers: Unseen Life on Earth*. Washington, D.C.: American Society for Microbiology Press, 2000.

Wakeford, Tom. *Liaisons of Life: From Hornworts to Hippos, How the Unassuming Microbe Has Driven Evolution*. New York: John Wiley & Sons, 2001.

Internet Addresses

American Society for Microbiology. *Microbe World*.
http://www.microbeworld.org/

Dennis Kunkel Microscopy, Inc. ©2005.
http://www.denniskunkel.com/

Quill Graphics. *Cells Alive!* ©1994-2006.
http://www.cellsalive.com/

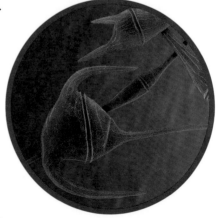

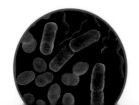

Index

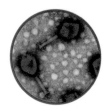